JOURNEY

Fred Benton Holmberg

Fred Benton Holmberg

Illustrated by Lori Russell

DURRELL PUBLICATIONS
DISTRIBUTED BY
The Stephen Greene Press
P. O. BOX 1000
BRATTLEBORO, VERMONT

SBN: 911764-10-0
SECOND PRINTING
Designer: Faith Nicholas
Printed and Bound by Jenkins-Universal
United States of America

TABLE OF CONTENTS

JOURNEY

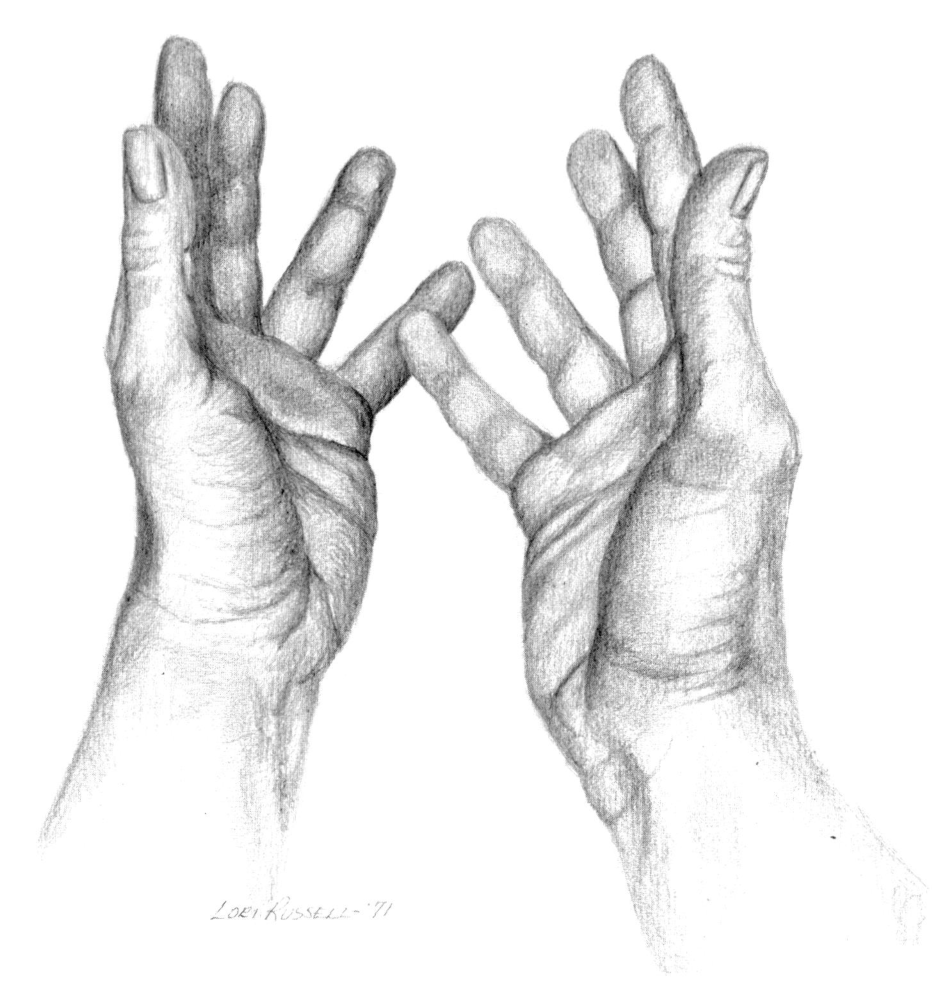
LORI RUSSELL-'71

JOURNEY IN

Who am I?

Each time that I think I have the answer, I discover that there is still more to find. I seem to be an unfolding, a continuous process of unfolding that had no beginning and has no end.

The Journey In is the beautiful and the ugly, the painful and the proud unfolding of who I am. That fact is not profound. It is simply true.

ECCE!

To behold is
  to stand within yourself
And see
  another stand within himself
And know that
  both are standing in the same place.

To behold is
  to feel another's feeling
And find
  it to be so much like your own
That you know
  within two are one.

To behold is
  to journey together
  parallel, yet enfolded
  held close, yet wide open.

To behold is
  to give to the other
  all that he needs
  out of the fullness
  that you are.
  no more, no less.

To behold is
  to live wildly this day
  to hope joyfully for tomorrow,
  never to yearn for
    what might have been
    and can never be.

SO . . . . BEHOLD!!!

RAIN

THE rain has always moved me
  The feelings
  The memories
  The dreams.

The rain has always moved me.
  Not to tears
  But laughter,
  Warm and gentle
  Running like an overflowing brook.

The rain has always moved me.
  I skied the rain.
  Snow beneath my feet,
  Rain against my face,
  Cold and warm, a good feeling.

The rain has always moved me.
  Beside the angry ocean
  Behind frantic windshield wipers,
  Beating against the roof
  And I lying there.

The rain has always moved me.
  To think
  To feel
  To know
  To live.

The rain has always moved me
  Closer
  To life
  To fullness
  To you.

SKY THOUGHTS

Sky and sun and space,
Beyond a limitless existence.
Churning, shades and silences
Within, a caldron of emotion.

How to reach beyond from within,
I do not know.
I feel, sometimes die or live
But all within.

No-one knows within,
Perhaps not even I.
A prison, a retreat?
Who or what holds the key?

A Smile, a quip, a kind remark
Hiding all the darkness
Yet ever there,
Confined, imprisoned within.

Sky and sun and space
I need you. I cry for you.
I reach and fall and reach again.
How to get beyond, from within?

DECISION

How can I tell you how I feel?
Emotions that tear like saw teeth
Jagged, raw, relentless and numbing
Yet bringing pain, deep and lasting.

How can I tell you what I think?
When thoughts pour out of a cone
Overflowing from some endless center
Ever widening, reaching out from the deep.

How can I tell you who I am?
Ten thousand people, a single body
That masks so neatly the colors and
The shades of who and what I am.

How can I tell you, of impending death
For like a child, struggling for first breath
I am about to die to the warmth of an old womb
To be born again in the glaring scorch of the soul.

How can I tell you . . . the frightening dreams
That drive me to return to what I was:
The fear of loneliness, the need for love
Yet pulled beyond where I have been.

How can I tell you?
Can you hear me?
Can you see?
Can I?

DEPARTURE

God, with long grey beard and flowing robe
Christ, with gentle hands and mystic face
Holy Spirit, Hallowe'en ghost in theological garb,
Church, building with need of paint and heat
I leave you to rust and eternal decay.

Universal pull and demand upon my life,
Jesus, flesh and bone, rough and real
Unnamed communication between all being
People with passions for justice and peace
I join with you, not with answers but with searchings.

World of words with long lost meanings
World of rituals ancient and obscure
World of masks and phony voices
I struggle to be free, for I have been with you long.

World of actions that bind up wounds
World of touchings, warm, cold, but real
World of burning openness
I struggle to be part of you. It is not easy.

ONE DROP OF RED

Black and white
  and shades of grey
Broken only by a drop of red
  where death and despair
  bring life's only color.
Faces, seagulls, angles, form
  all blend as one
No one by himself
  except in desperation.
Life, a series of grey
  duties and pretenses.
The only judgement being
  he who acts it best.
Give me
One drop of red,
Even death and despair
If that will give me life
Other than the grey.

BLOSSOM

I AM not a
Seller of boards
And bricks
Fashioned into
forms, called houses.

I am a
Dreamer of dreams
A feeler of
the Universe
A blossom
of Eternity.

I am a writer
of Songs,
A teller of tales
A mind capable
of revealing
the universe to
the unseeing.

So why do I hide
And pretend that
Money is more
important than ideas
and Houses and
Cottages and
Ski Lodges
and spend my life
Supporting bricks
and Boards
Fashioned into
forms called houses?

What is wrong with
me? What happened
or was it all a sham
a cover for what
was real?
I cannot believe
that I was destined
for any less
than a blossom
of eternity.
Therefore I must
cease to do
those things
which put frost on
the blossom of
eternity
and turn to death
life
before it has unfolded.

LIFE

Life is never down or up but always moving in more
directions than the eye can see or
the heart can feel.

"I"

THEY tell me about my feelings
in tones and phrases
that make me feel
less than I am.

Yet my heart cries out, how
can any man's feelings
be more or less
than they are?

They make me hide beauty in black folders
and encase eternal dreams
in wax paper
and in shadows.

They buy what isn't me
and think that they have purchased
a corner of my being
for a few dollars.
And I wonder about them....
But they are not the problem.

I know now, who I am.
I have the courage to be just that.
So I will take the beauty out of black folders,
And proclaim my passion and celebrate my living
For I, not they, am the only hindrance to my being.

ONE

WE are all One.

One with ourselves
One with each other
One with All.

To be One is
to hold with arms wide open
to drink deeply – yet always replenish
to celebrate everything – even grief.

I am One !
One with myself
One with you
One with All.

I am One with
Him who is the eternal – at both ends
Her who brings music when all else is silence
Them who are laughter and tears all intermingled.

and strangely enough
it matters not
if anyone knows this
because I know it !

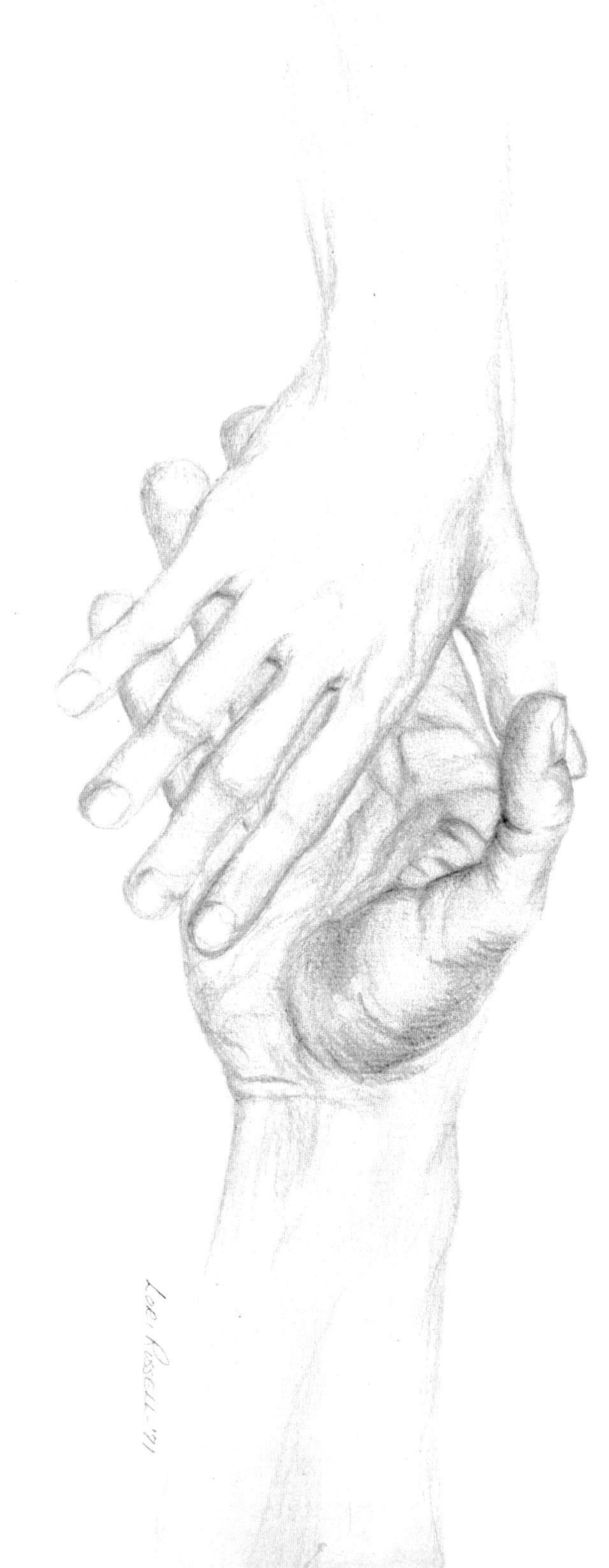

JOURNEY OUT

Who are you?

That is not easy to discover. You are from my point of view only what you let me see. You are of course much more than that, at least a thousand shades of being and I see only a few shades and even fewer shadows.

You touch my life with your gentle brushings and your agonizing stabs. Often times, at the moment of your touching, I was totally unaware of the impact of the encounter. The impact of the touching remains with me still.

Strangely enough, as I have reached out to you I have also reached in to new unfoldings of myself.

For that I am deeply grateful.

THE LANGUAGE OF MAN

To speak the language of man
Is to be able to read
A smile
And see the joy
Or the cover up for hurt
Or the blank pasted on
Feeling of non-existence.

To speak the language of man
Is to be able to laugh
Openly
And at yourself
And sense the comedy
Of two people playing together
Or two blades of grass.

To speak the language of man
Is to be able to hear
The silence
And let its thunder
Send vibrations through
Your being, as you
Contemplate your oneness.

To speak the language of man
Is to be able to cry
Alone
Or with another
And let the tears be for joy
Or for inescapable sadness
And sometimes not know which.

To speak the language of man
Is to be able to touch
Another
With hands in your pocket
Or wrapped tightly around them
Knowing that touching has
Nothing to do with the physical.

To speak the language of man
Is to be able to find
Anyone
And everyone
And to know that you and they
Are the same in everything
That really matters to each one.

To speak the language of man
Is to read . . . and laugh . . . and hear
. . . and cry . . . and touch . . .
And find
And know that if you speak it
. . . You are!

FLIGHT

You, too, are airborne now,
Flying, one to meet the other,
Yet joined in pulse and fibre
And one in inner longing.

Fire burns within me
Seeking touch and tender kiss.
Passion unleashed in abandon
Welded into one eternal being.

Time and space draws us nearer.
Yesterdays lose their meanings.
To see and hold and blend
And give life to one another.

Gentle, tender, strong
Moving in single pattern
One love between us.

I do not seek to understand
Or analyze . . . . .
Only to feel the joy,
Live the moment
Be, who I am!

MEETING

SHE came as a drop of water comes
Fashioned by clouds in the early morning sky.
She clung for a moment to the spill of a pine
And sparkled like a diamond crystal in the warm sun.

We met there in the pine
Two drops of water
That became one
Utterly together.

The weight of our being set us loose from the pine
And we fell between earth and sky.
The sun made new colors within and around us
And life at last was full and strong and gentle.

The earth met us beneath the pine
And drank deeply
Of our being,
Our oneness.

I live now in the earth, on the ground
And I look toward the pine
And the early morning rain
Wanting and waiting,
Yet I cannot find her
For we have been absorbed
By the earth.
Forever a part of each other.
Forever lost to each other.

I WANT THEM TO KNOW

I WANT them to know
That I am loved;
Not by children
Who drink so often
Beyond even the dryness;
Not by old women
Whose sons have deserted them;
Not by young women
Whose passions lie unfilled;
I want them to know
That I am loved
By you who fills
My cup
To overflowing.

KAREN

SHE said, "It is for you."
A soft paper, red and green.
Her imprint was upon it.

Leaves with strong veins,
Featherlike sheets of grass.
Textured patterns of life.

It looked like lace and leaves
Arranged by some magic hand.
The magic was Karen.

Warm child in a cold world
Who sees beyond her time,
Who touches life and turns it.

Bright child in a dim world
Whose eyes are the blue of sky and sea,
Who moves in rhythms that are eternal.

My child, yet not really.
Child of eternal dream
Child for eternity's unborn hopes.

Karen, warm child of life
Who sees a world we are blind to see.
I thank you for your gift.

TO SHELDON DAVID GOLDMAN

on the day
of his
BAR MITZVAH

Boy, Man.
Two words,
Close in meaning and in feeling.
Separated by celebration
And a holy gathering.

Boy, Man.
The world of childhood
So warm and tender.
You have lived it with
An infinite sense of beauty.
Your childhood,
Your boy time
Has touched us
Because you have touched us
And we have seen in the boy
All the marks of a man being born.

Boy, Man.
The world of manhood
Calls you beyond where you have stood,
Making new demands upon all your life.
Yet we know that you will answer well
For we have shared in what you have already been.

Boy, Man.
Sheldon David.
We welcome you to the world of men
Where strength can be measured by tenderness,
And courage journeys with caring;
Where wisdom reflects Eternal light
And holiness an Eternal joy.

Boy, Man.
Sheldon David
We love you
For all that you have been,
For everything you are this day
And for all that you shall ever be.

TRAFFIC

Black man, sitting on white bridge
Who are you and where are you from?
Cars pass, people pass, busses pass
You sit there all alone,
Looking, searching. I wonder?

Do you know that I am looking too?
White on the outside
Black within . . . waiting to see
and understand . . . and yet, afraid
For if I see you and you see me
We can no longer hide from each other.

Black man sitting on white bridge
Will I walk over to you?
Or you to me?
Or will the traffic between
Snuff out one of our lives
And leave the other
Looking, searching, wondering?

FRIEND (1)

To be who you are
Will never be easy.

To dare to live the passion
That is within your being.

Will always bring tears
And sometimes ridicule.

Yet all that you are
Will burst the walls about you

And the passion will ride forth
Soaring like the eagles, tender as doves.

Yet ever in the shadow
I shall stand

With strength for the taking,
courage for the journey,
passion for new bornings.

So be all that you are.
Dare to live

So that I and eternity
May kiss your joy
And fill your longing.

FRIEND (2)

SOMEWHERE
In the encounter
Between
Two human beings
There is a moment,
Resisted
At first
Then slowly
Approached,
When there beats
A single heart,
A solitary vibration
So in rhythm
That it is
Eternal.

The pain
Of that moment
Is surpassed
Only
By the joy
Of two people,
Set free
Yet bound together
Forever
In a vibration
From which
There is no turning
Back,
No escape.

At that moment
A man
Knows
What it means
To love
And be loved.
In that moment
He finds
No limits,
No restrictions.
For that moment
There are
No words
Adequate
To contain it.

I know
For I have
Come to the knowing
And felt
The anguish
And the pain
Yet found
The joy
So deep
That it could
Only be
Expressed
In the shedding
Of tears
And the shout of my soul.

LORI RUSSELL-71

JOURNEY WITH

Who are we?

Much of what we discover about ourselves and each other is discovered during times of intense, concentrated and continued communication.

It was in the spring of 1969 that four of us spent a concentrated amount of time together in Paris, Yugoslavia, Italy, Austria, Germany, and Switzerland. We rode in a small car, stayed in the same places, met the same people, yet each of us travelled a very different journey.

It was in the spring of 1970 that sixteen of us took a trip in a school bus, driving the five thousand, six hundred and forty miles from Maine to Panama. Eleven of the group were high school students. We lived in the bus, on top of it and around it. At times the feeling was very tight. In the closeness of such an adventure you either disintegrate or come alive. We are very much alive.

We met people as we had on other journeys. We failed some of the people we met as we failed ourselves. It was not so with others.

There is a new dimension beyond the I and the You that comes on a journey with other people. Give it no name. Call it a Journey With.

THE BEGINNING OF TOMORROW

THERE is a growing here,
Subtle, sometimes unseen
Except by the sensitive.
There is a loving here
Tender, expressed in
Language, often unfamiliar.
There is a happening here,
Strong in its pull
On the riders of the Rojo Grande.

Sixteen on a bus,
Reaching toward each other
And yet so far beyond.
Beyond to new encounters
With land as challenging
As the life it nourishes.
Beyond to children,
Ragged, desolate, standing,
Waiting for that which seldom comes.

You watch the riders
You see then touch the children
With tenderness as well as pesos.
You hear the subtle murmurings of all
That is eternal.
And you see them pick the flowers
And run high up in the mountains
And they press your hand to
Their heartbeat
And all you feel is the beating
Of your own heart.
For you have been touched by
These people of tomorrow.

And as you ride the desolation
Of a land that's dry and burning
And you see the other children
In the shacks and in the squalor
And you ride the Rojo Grande
With the children of your own land
You feel again the deep disturbing
Of your soul which cries in anguish
For the beginning of tomorrow
Needs the children of both nations.

Perhaps the journey of the Rojo Grande
Is the beginning of tomorrow.

Rojo Grande is the name given to the school bus that carried the sixteen of us on the journey through Central America. It means Big Red.

HAIKU
of
THE DESERT

Hot sun, open space
Dust beneath your feet, and yet
A coolness within.

Desert cactus why?
So thorny and foreboding.
Blossoms like jewels!

To stand all alone
Is not to be by yourself
But to be with All.

A road leading out
To beyond where you have been
Is like cool water.

HELD

HE stood there
Only two,
Dirty, ragged,
Nose running,
Shivering,
Not knowing why.

He took the pesos
And the gum
And the life savers
Given by tourista.

She stood there
Seventeen
Well clothed
Wealthy
Warm
Traveling through.

She gave the pesos
And the gum
And the life savers
Then herself.

Kneeling before him
She rolled up his sleeve,
Pressed her hand warm
And close to his,
Hugged his shoulders,
Erased the coldness.

He smiled,
She smiled.
They were both alive.

THE BURRO

THE burro
Is a little guy
Who carries more
Than his share,
Be it a bundle of
Sticks or the
Flank kicking
Body of a man.

My heart cries
For him, yet
He does not
Complain or shed
Tears. He walks
Along, carrying his
Load as if God
Had somehow
Given him the
Graciousness to bear
The burden of
Other men.

Little burro,
You are like
Some people I
Know who carry
More than their
Share of mankind's
Burdens and do
Not complain.
Yet I know they
Cry and perhaps
You are crying, too.

Kick up your heels
And shed yourself
Of the burdens
That kick you.
But never lose
The gentleness
That surely makes
You one of life's
Most noble creatures.

Strangely enough
Little burro, your
Master does not
Know that he is
Really your slave.
But that does not
Matter for you
Know, and still you
Bear his burden for him.

THE HITCHHIKERS

He stood there and I was ashamed.
He would not beg, men don't do that.
I could not look at him, I, less than a man.
He and the other two wanted a ride.
A simple request, heightened by three days of waiting.
We had a bus, sixteen occupying twenty eight places.
The vote was NO, and I died a bit.
Was it the hair, the smell, the difference?
I wonder now.
The vote was NO, and I abided it.

We are the church. That's a laugh.
Even the beggers won't beg at the church anymore.
We want comfort and no crowding.
They are hungry for more than food.
We are the church. May God never get tied up with us.

I have a boy and two girls
And maybe someday one of them
Will be waiting three days
In the heat, at the border,
Waiting for someone like us
And that someone will come
And pass and vote NO.

He stood there and I am still ashamed.
Not at the vote, but only of myself
For being less than what I know I am,
For abiding the vote.
I know better. It matters little what they know.
Three people will haunt the rest of my life.
I cry, not for them but for myself.

He thanked me for trying, and waved.
I cannot look, for I am still ashamed.

PARALLEL

Four people.
Four worlds.
One only brushing the next.
Each wrapped in shape and form,
Seen from the outside,
Never lived from within,
Except by one.

Glimpses shared.
Places together
Yet seen separately and alone,
Each holding a bank of memories.
Four people, we are
Living in four separate worlds.
Alone.

Judgements have no meaning.
My world judges yours,
Which makes no sense
In time or space
Or in our understanding.
Four people
Four worlds
Travelling together,
Yet in Parallel

Never one, separate, alone.
Four.

TOURIST BUSSES

"And on your left is this and that"
      The canned sardines crane their necks.
"And on your right is that and this"
      In rhythm turn to see the other side.

They leave the can as sheep.
      "Move quickly, dear, see it all"
As goats they climb the winding stairs
      "Ten minutes for the second floor."

"We leave tomorrow at seven sharp"
      Canned again in air-conditioned sweat.
"Look now, dearie, toward the river"
      The natives are so quaint this time of year.

The canned sardines, the herd of sheep
The climbing goats, the animated doll
Traveling in their air-conditioned isle
Think that they have seen it all.

Yet all that they have seen from inside
Is the insulated reflection of themselves.
Someday, somewhere, they will leave the cocoon
And touch and feel the world outside.

YUGOSLAVIA

DARK night, the road is black
Curving, bumping, through foreign wood.
Light behind drawn curtains,
Language strange and deep
Bring feelings of mystery
Alone and yet together.

Dark wood and sturdy tables
Stolen glances, whispers from dim-lit corners
Yet shining eyes of waitress
Belie the need herein
And leave us wondering,
Alone and yet together.

Daylight and glistening mountains
Cable car ascent like shooting star
Laughter and smell of last night's dinner
Clinging to today's ski clothes
Pleasant eyes and gracious offers
Bring new life
Together now and not alone.

Chairlift swinging in bright sun
Yells and shouts of fullfilled dreams
Sliding skis and graceful motions
At last a sense of being
Warm beyond the sun,
Inside and secure.

Days ending, language barrier broken
Descending stars, now as one together
Laughter, warmth and farewell
Same room . . . new light
Life reaching out beyond tables
Only men together, not alone.

NO TEARS

WHY should I cry?
For myself, for you,
For us all ?

We have learned
To make monuments of
War and blood.

And hold celebrations
And gatherings of men
Sanctified by priestly blessings.

Even the cold of heart
Are stirred by inner
Memories, dreams, despairs.

Why should I cry ?
Not for the dead
But for the living.

For the memories
Erase the horrors
And the monstrosities
Become monuments
And we move again
In same old patterns.

I cry for us all
For in a thousand years
We are still the same.

Tomorrow is another day.
Tomorrow is another war.
Tomorrow ? I cry for today.

GRAVESIDE

Soldier why ?
A question not to ask.
"Gefallen in Italien"
"Died in Italy"
Two languages, one death.
Two mothers, one heartbreak.
Two dreams, one nightmare.
Soldier why ?
A question not to ask.
Strong men, young men
Full of life, now broken.
Good years ended,
Bringing death to each other.
Uncommon faces, common blood.
Soldier why ?
A question not to ask.

NOTRE DAME —THE WINDOW

WINDOW, how black you look without
Three statues marring even your form
White stone makes perfect pattern
But you are black and nothing more.

Within you are color and life
Standing in awe and adoration
Rose of many shades and variations
Holding memories of a trillion glances
You are alive as if only the rays of daylight
Could give you life and breath and feel.

Black window, how will I know you
Unless I am willing to walk within
Yet once inside I may forget
Your blackness from without.

Window of Notre Dame, you are life
Other men's shades seen as blackness
Yet from within colorful,
Rich with life and meaning.

Window of Notre Dame let me always
See you from without and within

That I may see
The blackness and color
Of my own life
And yours.

LORI RUSSELL-

JOURNEY BEYOND

Who will ask the final question?

When is a man born and when does a man die? Is eternity at both ends of life? Have we always been? Will we always be?

For hundreds of thousands of years man was confined to the earth. He dreamed of flight and space but his feet were bound to the ground, except in the tales of his Gods. Now he walks on the moon. Where will he walk tomorrow? Perhaps he has always travelled in space and was only bound to this planet by the physical limits of his undeveloped mind. Who knows the answer?

Where does it all end and where does it all begin? Questions, questions, questions!

My life has been touched, no matter how gently, by all human life that has ever been. My life will touch, no matter how minutely, all that will ever be. That is surely the beginning of beyond.

I have died many times and birth seems to be a continual process in my being. Other men's borning and dying has surely added dimension to my own.

The Journey Beyond is a part of the eternity at both ends of life. CELEBRATE IT!

GOING

It happened in the cold light of day.
Was it afternoon or morning ?
Time made little difference.
He presided at his own funeral.
No great crowds
Or flowers or music.
Just the loneliness that death always is.

He felt it coming.
A call or a beckoning ?
Something he knew would happen.
And when it came it was all right.
No need for sadness or tears.
He thought he should cry himself.
After all, everyone does
But there was no need for tears.

He wanted to reach back across the death line
To tell her she had made it possible for him to die.
Most people creep toward death.
He sang toward it.
He wanted to reach back across the death line
To tell her again of her love alone
That made his life fully alive.
Even the short moments became eternities of loving.

Now he stands in a new world.
A new time, another place.
And the shades of those moments in that other life
Caress his being
And hold him toward the future.

He is gone now . . . beyond himself as he was.
Do not weep for him.
Sing for him.

Sing songs that have no death boundaries.
Dance dances that swirl across mountains.
Live - as long as forever is!

For to grieve or die
Would hold him back from the future
That is beyond his dying.

THE PUBLIC PASSION AND THE PRIVATE POISON

(for Martin Luther King, Jr.)

WHILE men with broken hearts and shame filled spirits
poured out their grief in tears and anguished cries,
Other men, in silent glee,
exulted in his death;
roamed and raced to fan the flames
of violence and looting greed.

While men, who long since had soared beyond the bonds
of color, marched arm in arm with torn,
yet determined hearts,
Other men, pious pilgrims,
shed their tears;
said their prayers,
and thought, "I have done enough."

While a nation, bowed, broken, humbled from within,
paused to honor a life of greatness and turn anew to
greater tasks,
Little men whispered,
with arrogance and pride
their shameless words of hate.
"He was a Commie to be sure!"

While One wept, and bent down again to lift
a shattered soul, slain with coldness and so young;
life but half lived,
A man shouted Nigger,
and clenched his fist
to smash and destroy again
the birth of an eternal dream.

T'was ever thus.
    When night is darkest, the thunder rolls
        to echo the hollowness and evil deeds of men.
    While some men come with light,
        other men come to bring an even darker night.
And yet, it has always been,
    not the public passion or even the private poison,
    but the light of one man that has chased away the
        darkness of even our darkest night.

FOR MARION

You turned on the lights
And our life is brighter because of it.

You pushed your dreams for children
Through the sluggish halls of state
And widened the horizons for years to come.

You pulled us out of ivory towers
And prodded us when we talked of love
And loved but little.

Your feet walked through doors of poverty
and hurt . . . when our own had become leaden masses
Unmoved and without feeling.

You made us angry because you
wouldn't let us avoid the mirror you held before us.

You were torn apart
      yet you mended.
You were sick, yet overcame it.
You refused to let life rule you . . . .
Rather you brought to life
a strong sense of living.

Your eyes beheld the future
Your hopes encompassed the family of man
And we loved you, every prod, every push, every pull . . .

Because we knew that, somehow, because of you, life
would be fuller for children, richer for
ourselves, more hopeful for the human family.

And so, Marion, wherever you are, will you join somehow
in our celebration of your life . . . .
We salute you
We celebrate you
We love you.

FOR ROBERT

ONLY the strongest of men
can be truly warm and tender and gentle.
You were surely that.

Only the securest of men
can afford the luxury of never passing
judgement on one's fellow beings.
You were surely that.

Only the bravest of men
never allows the burden of pain
to erase the joy and the laughter of life.
You were surely that.

And so it has been through your days.

While some men tried to prove their manliness
You were simply a man.

While some men ripped and tore and gossipped
You understood life and accepted
each of us for what we are . . . . no more, no less.

While some men whined that life had treated them
ill and cried out in agony and despair
You took what life you had
lived it, loved it
breathed through it all the strength
of your being . . . .

And we who stand now on your other side
Know that we are richer still
Because of what you were
And will always be.

FOR AUNT GLADYS

"The morning of her death/life"

We reached the top of the mountain
And her spirit whispered all around us.
We soared across the whiteness
And her laughter echoed through us.
We came to a sudden halt in the meadow
And in the sunlight she seemed to
Stand there with us.
And there together
We knew that Aunt Gladys
was all right
And as alive as she had ever been.

So weep not, but rather
Celebrate
Celebrate the tallness of her life
and the reaching out.
Celebrate the quietness of her
life and the gentle brushing.

Celebrate the integrity of her life
and the struggle
to be true
and honest
and caring
Celebrate all that she was and is.

And know that your own life
Has been richer
Because her life and your life
met and intermingled
and touched each other
deeply.

In the early morning
When the ocean touches the shore
know that her spirit whispers with it.

In the heat of noonday
When life seems hard or tired
Know that her laughter brings a cooling breeze.
At sunset when the shadows lengthen
Give thanks to God
for the eternity
that binds us with her
forever.

TO CHUCK

SOMEWHERE in the early morning of eternity
you are running free.
Loosed from the bonds of earth
Unchained from all that bound you here.

The years together were too brief,
Yet who is to measure time?
Or how long is long enough?

You brought so much joy
And whispered so much hope
To those who loved you most.

Gentle sharings of all that mattered.
The courage to run when most men would walk.
Passionate concerns for the lonely and the lost.
A mind sharpened by life and warmed by love.

We watched you
And loved you
And rejoiced in your being.

We celebrated with you
And for you
And waited for your life
To unfold and to blossom.

A single thread
of darkness
or loneliness
pulled you beyond
to the moment of now.

We cannot fully understand
Nor shall we try . . . .

We simply know that somewhere
    in the vastness of all that is
You are running free
And the ocean of eternity cools your feet
As you run unhampered on the sands of all tomorrows.
And a lone seagull calls to you
And you respond with laughter.

You carry now, no burden,
No chain or bond to hold you
You carry only the warmth
and the love
of those who cared

So run free
And open your arms
And touch the clouds
and dance with the morning sun
And know that even in our tears
    we celebrate with you
And bid you good journey
Till we meet again tomorrow.

PARTING

(morning of the first "moon walk")

EARTH, you are my mother, so warm and gentle.
Earth, you are my father, so stern, demanding.
Earth, my parents, I leave you.

I know not where I go.
Am I being sent or called ?
I fly to yonder moon and then
Beyond to other planets, stars, and dreams.

Someday, perhaps I shall return to you, earth.
Someday, perhaps I shall come back.
But not as I journeyed forth.
I am full grown now.

There is no place from which I am barred because of age.
Destiny calls to me from beyond the telescopes, and
Cameras may not record my wanderings.

Venus, Mars, Jupiter, or some other unnamed place
in unseen galaxies call to me and I will heed their call.
My life demands it !

Earth, O earth, my Mother, so warm and gentle.
Earth, O earth, my Father, so stern, demanding.
Earth, small cradle of my first beginnings.
I, Man, must leave you now.

Last minute doubtings.
Have I learned my lessons?
Perhaps I shouldn't leave?
Doubt always seeks to conquer dreams.
But I am a dreamer
And beyond the moon . . . . .

Earth, my Mother, warm and gentle
Earth, my Father, stern, demanding
Goodbye.

AT CLOSING

and

FOR NEW BEGINNINGS

this book is dedicated to

ERIC, KAREN, and KRISTEN
who both share the journey
and continue it

and to YOU who find
in the journey

LIGHT for the taking . . . .